MW01526333

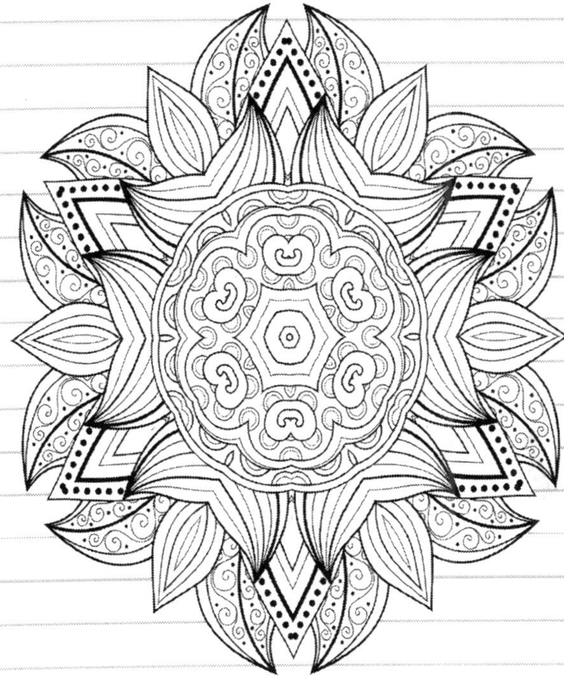

ZenMaster Coloring Books

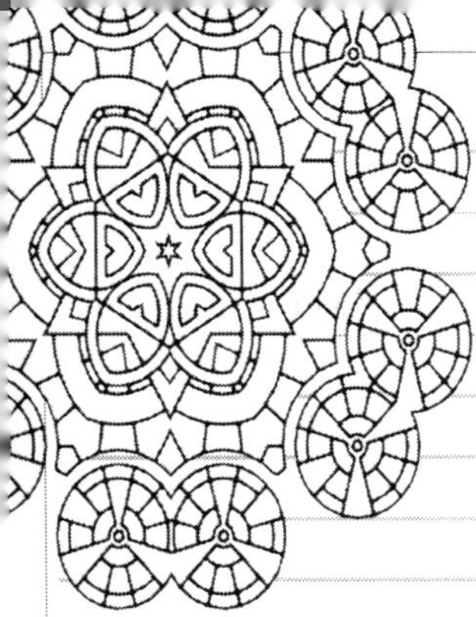

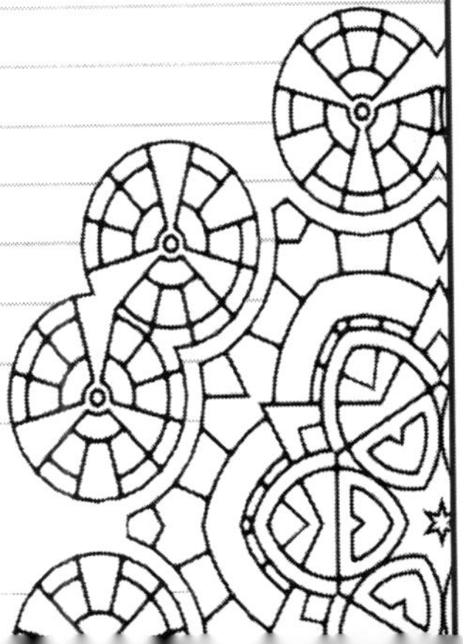

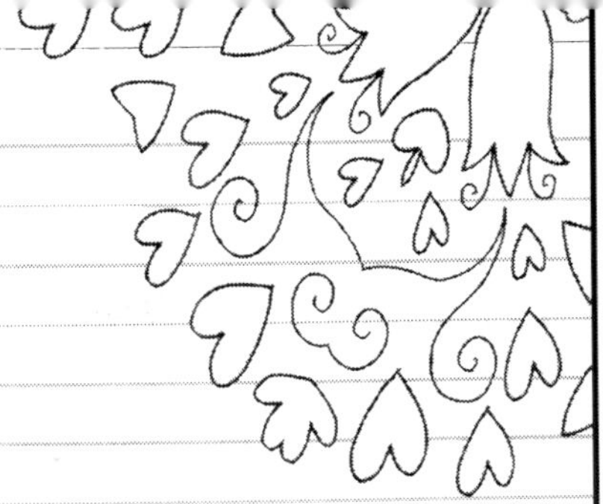

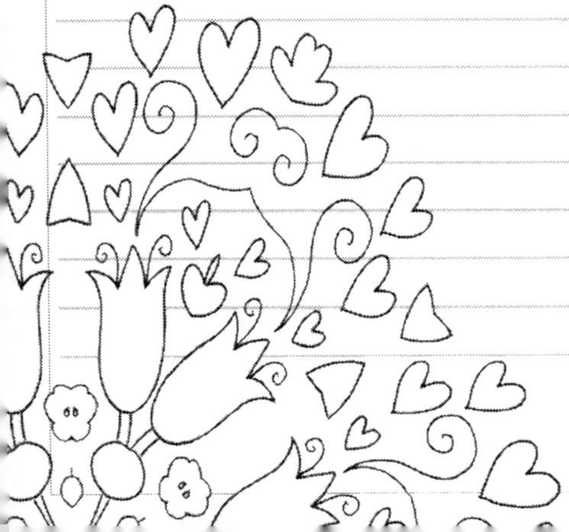

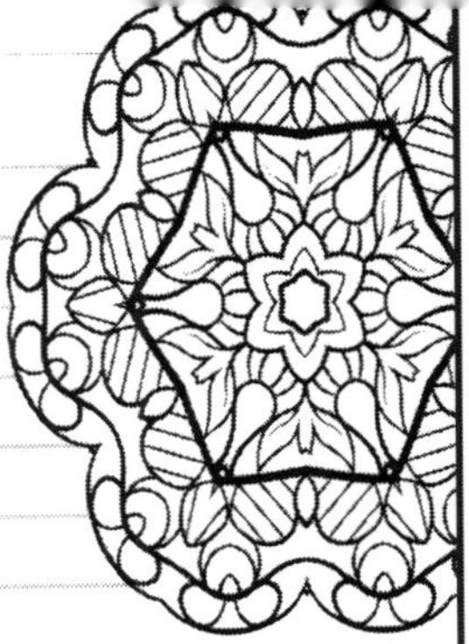

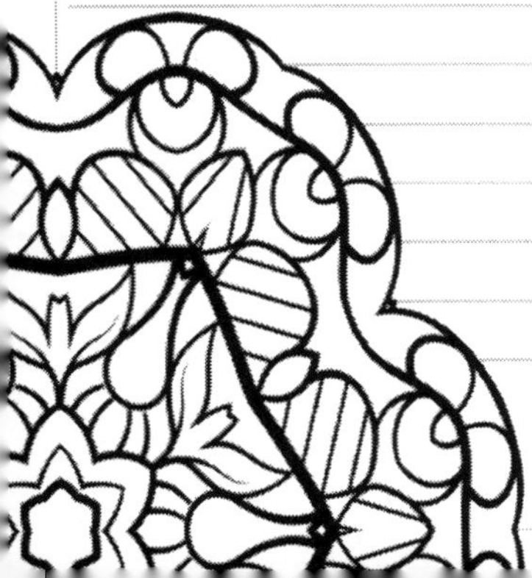

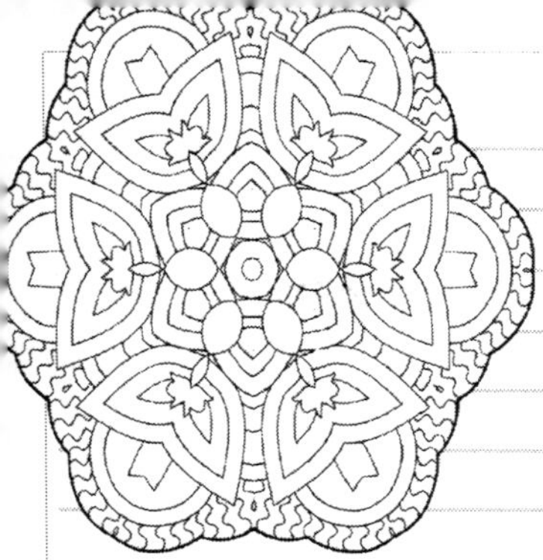

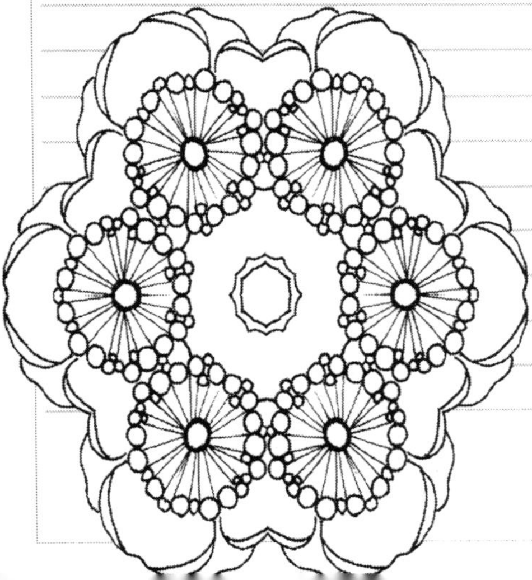

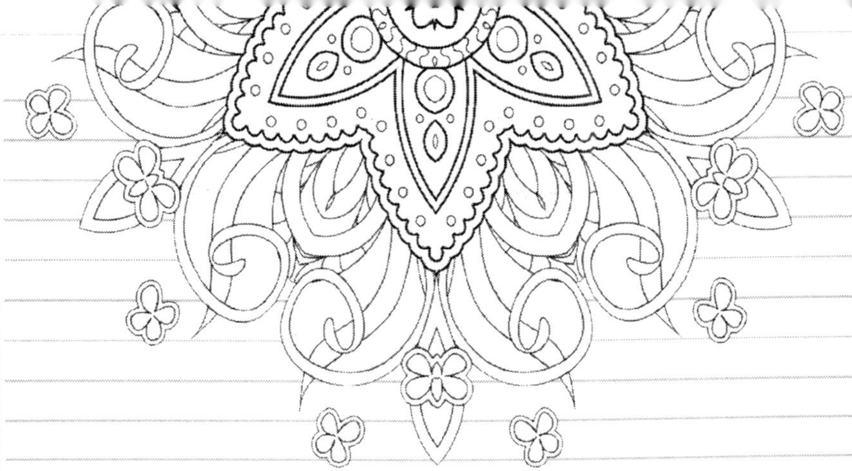

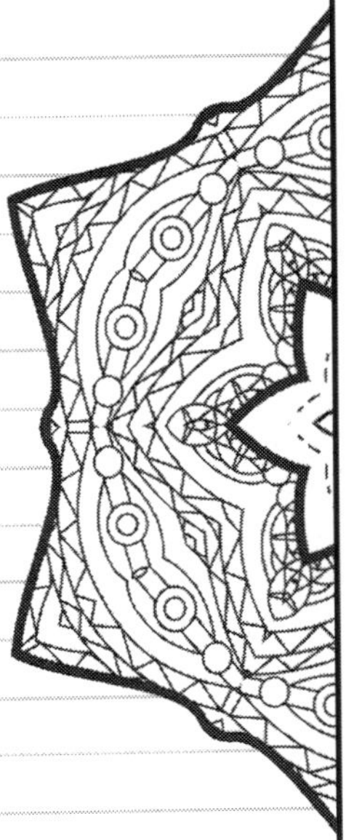

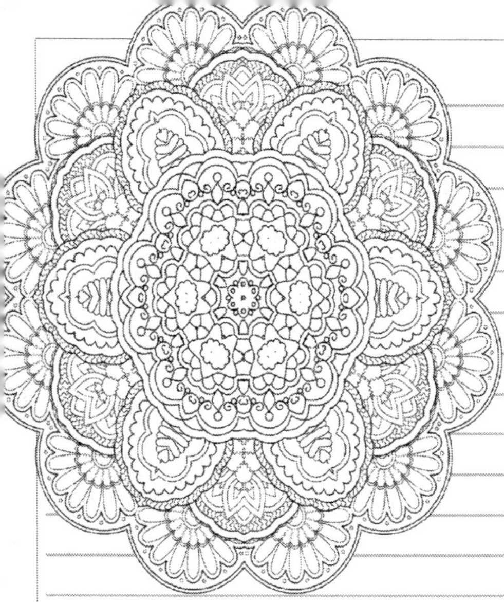

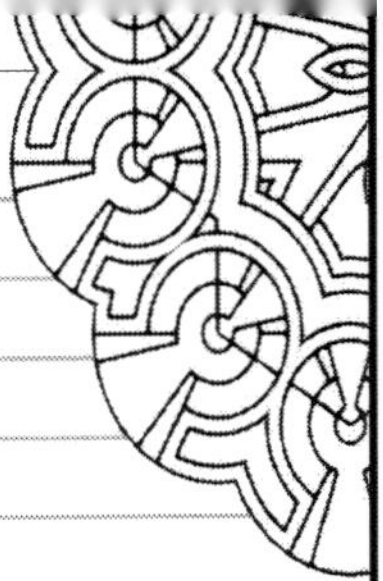

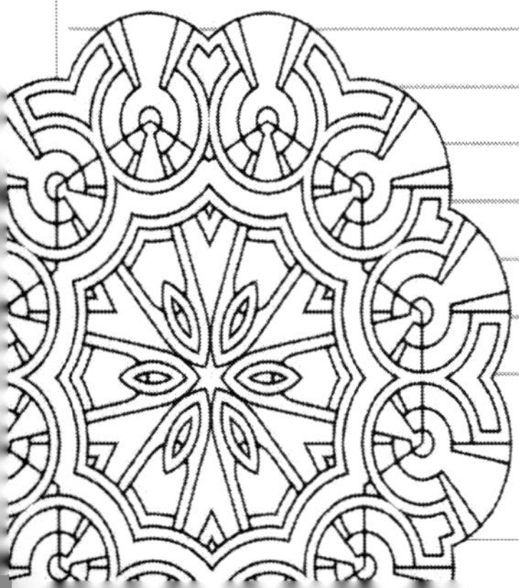

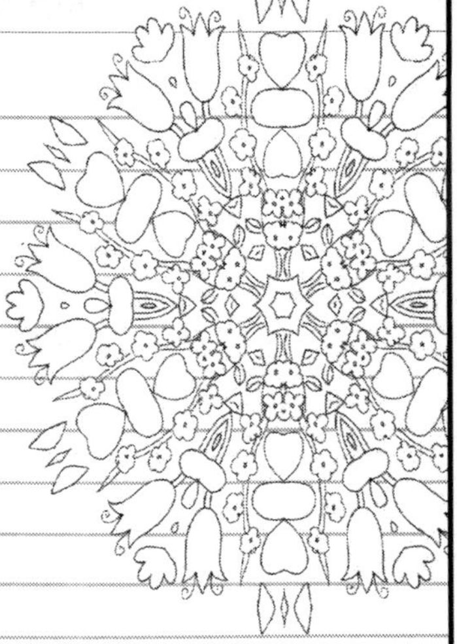

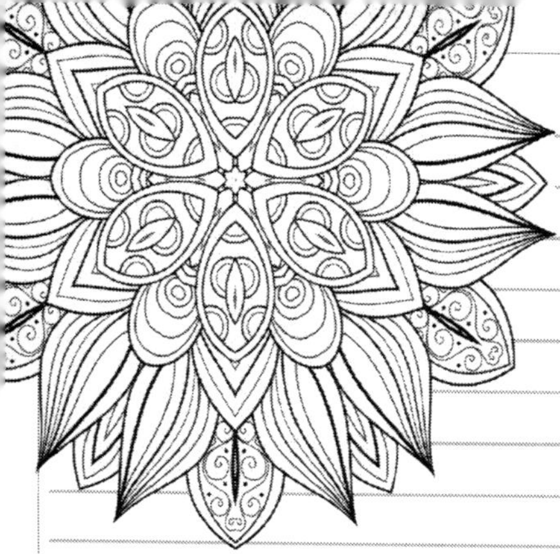

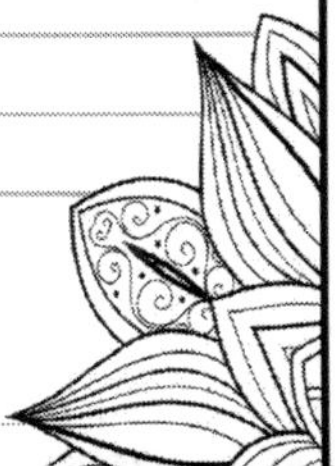

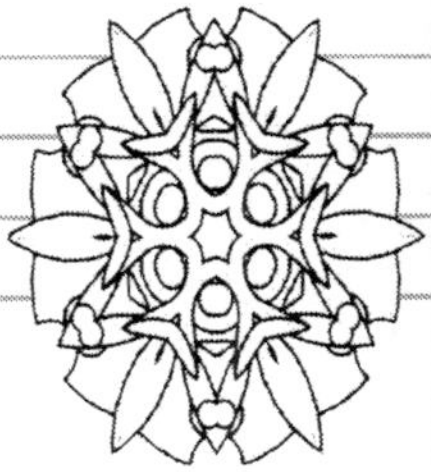

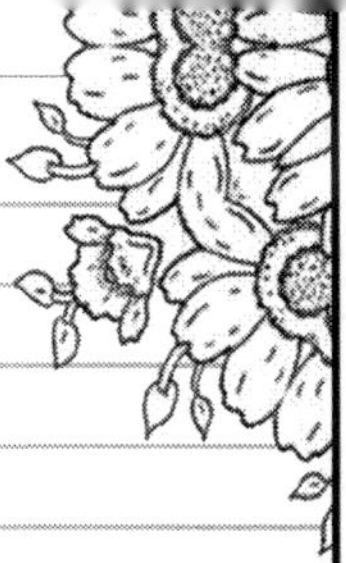

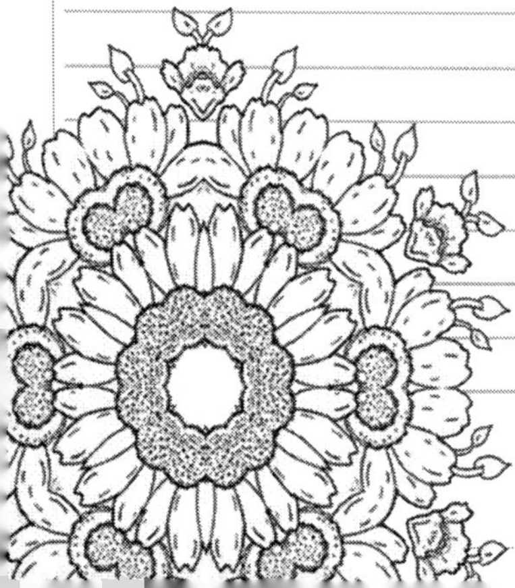

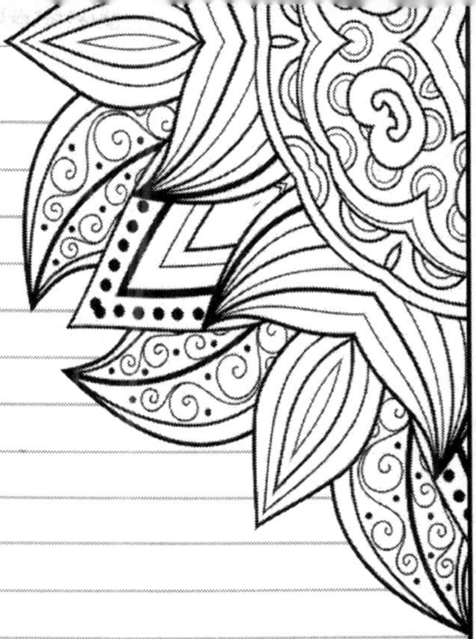

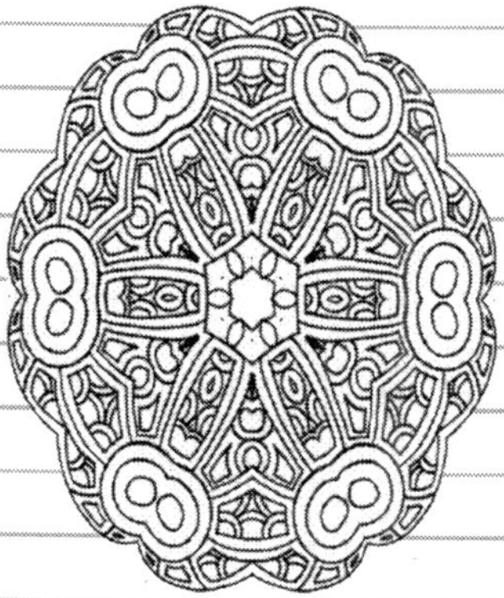

96028655R00057

Made in the USA
Columbia, SC
19 May 2018